THIS BOOK BELONGS TO

_____

CONTENT

If a girl looks swell when she meets you, who gives a damn if she's late? Nobody.

Jerome D.Salinger

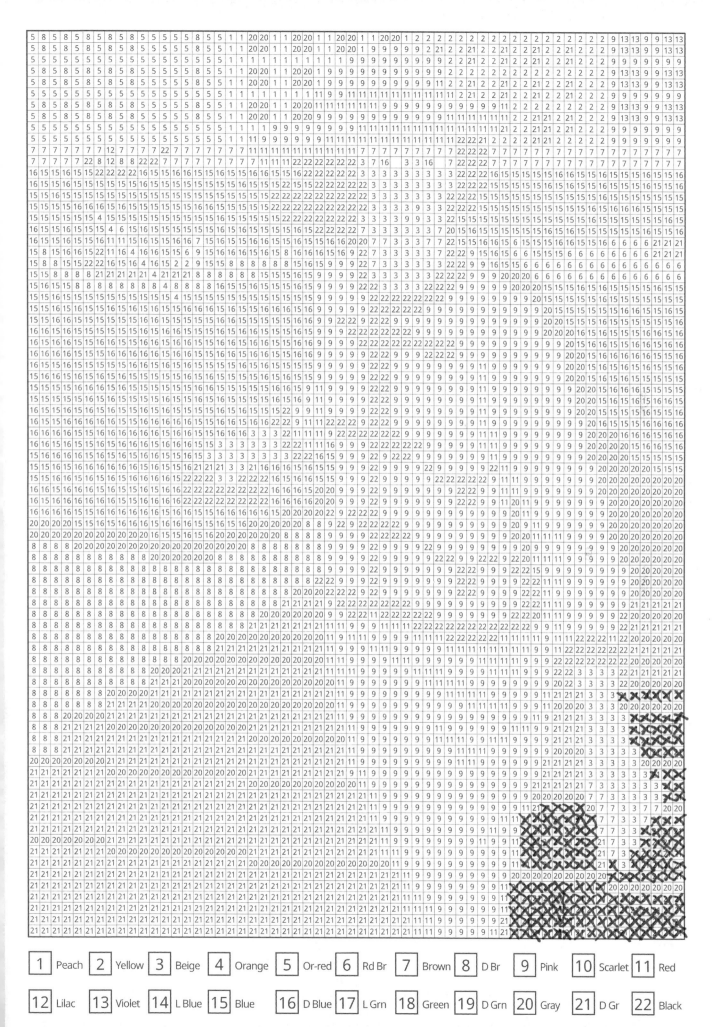

| 1 | Peach | 2 | Yellow | 3 | Beige | 4 | Orange | 5 | Or-red | 6 | Rd Br | 7 | Brown | 8 | D Br | 9 | Pink | 10 | Scarlet | 11 | Red |
| 12 | Lilac | 13 | Violet | 14 | L Blue | 15 | Blue | 16 | D Blue | 17 | L Grn | 18 | Green | 19 | D Grn | 20 | Gray | 21 | D Gr | 22 | Black |

There are three things men can do with women: love them, suffer for them, or turn them into literature.

Stephen Stills

1	Peach	2	Yellow	3	Beige	4	Orange	5	Or-red	6	Rd Br	7	Brown	8	D Br	9	Pink	10	Scarlet	11	Red
12	Lilac	13	Violet	14	L Blue	15	Blue	16	D Blue	17	L Grn	18	Green	19	D Grn	20	Gray	21	D Gr	22	Black

Being a woman is a terribly difficult task, since it consists principally in dealing with men.

Joseph Conrad

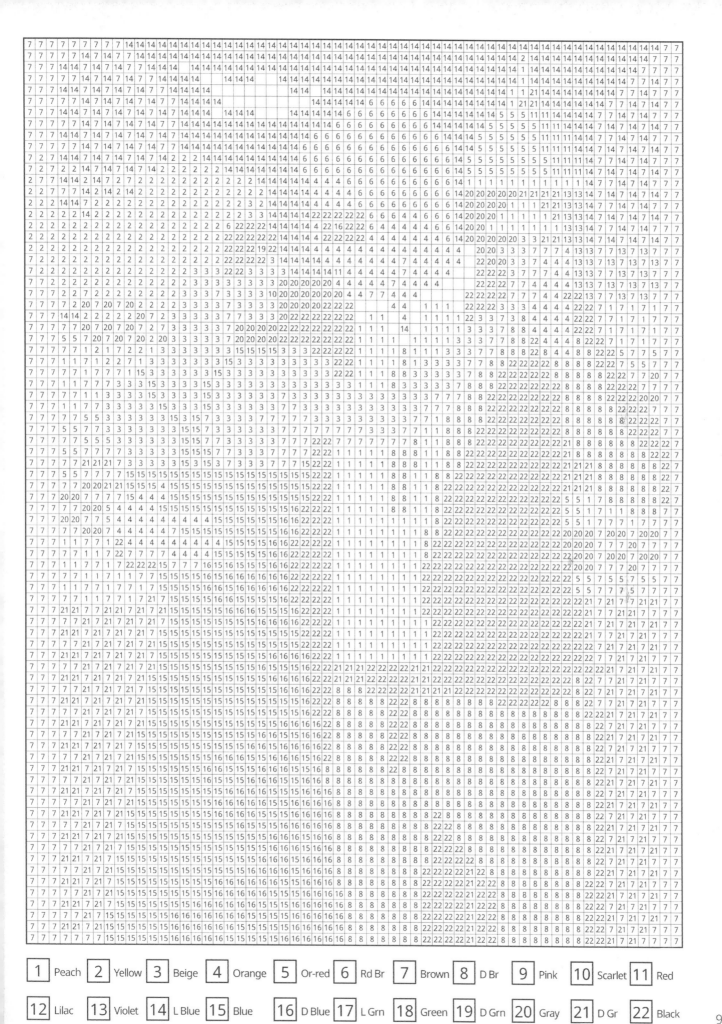

Adornment, what science!
Beauty, what a weapon!
Modesty, what elegance!

Coco Chanel

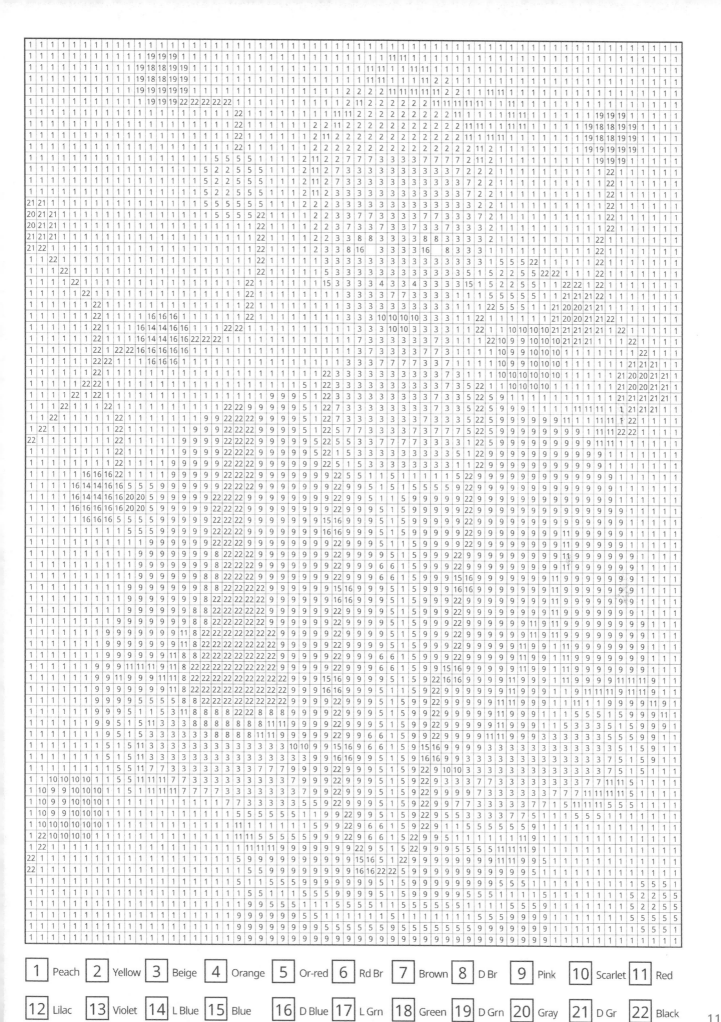

| 1 Peach | 2 Yellow | 3 Beige | 4 Orange | 5 Or-red | 6 Rd Br | 7 Brown | 8 D Br | 9 Pink | 10 Scarlet | 11 Red |

| 12 Lilac | 13 Violet | 14 L Blue | 15 Blue | 16 D Blue | 17 L Grn | 18 Green | 19 D Grn | 20 Gray | 21 D Gr | 22 Black |

11

*When God makes
a beautiful woman,
the devil opens a new
register.*

Ambrose Bierce

1 Peach 2 Yellow 3 Beige 4 Orange 5 Or-red 6 Rd Br 7 Brown 8 D Br 9 Pink 10 Scarlet 11 Red

12 Lilac 13 Violet 14 L Blue 15 Blue 16 D Blue 17 L Grn 18 Green 19 D Grn 20 Gray 21 D Gr 22 Black

Lots of people want to ride with you in the limo, but what you want is someone who will take the bus with you when the limo breaks down.

Oprah Winfrey

| 1 | Peach | 2 | Yellow | 3 | Beige | 4 | Orange | 5 | Or-red | 6 | Rd Br | 7 | Brown | 8 | D Br | 9 | Pink | 10 | Scarlet | 11 | Red |
| 12 | Lilac | 13 | Violet | 14 | L Blue | 15 | Blue | 16 | D Blue | 17 | L Grn | 18 | Green | 19 | D Grn | 20 | Gray | 21 | D Gr | 22 | Black |

15

Women want love to be a novel, men a short story.

Daphne du Maurier

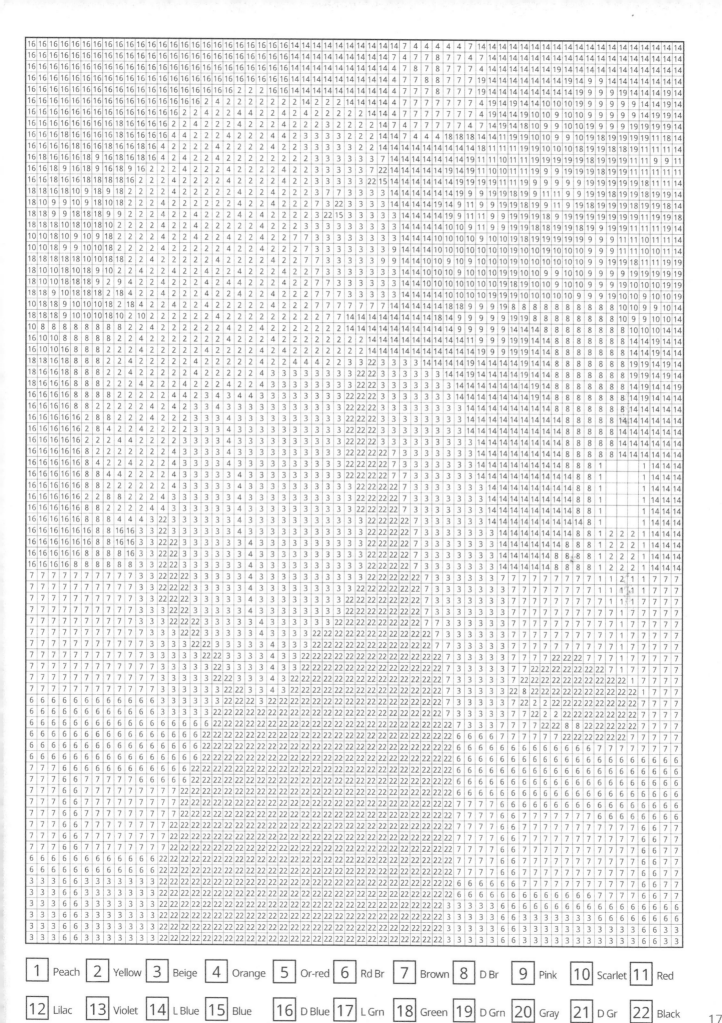

A woman asks little
of love: only that she
be able to feel like
a heroine.

Mignon McLaughlin

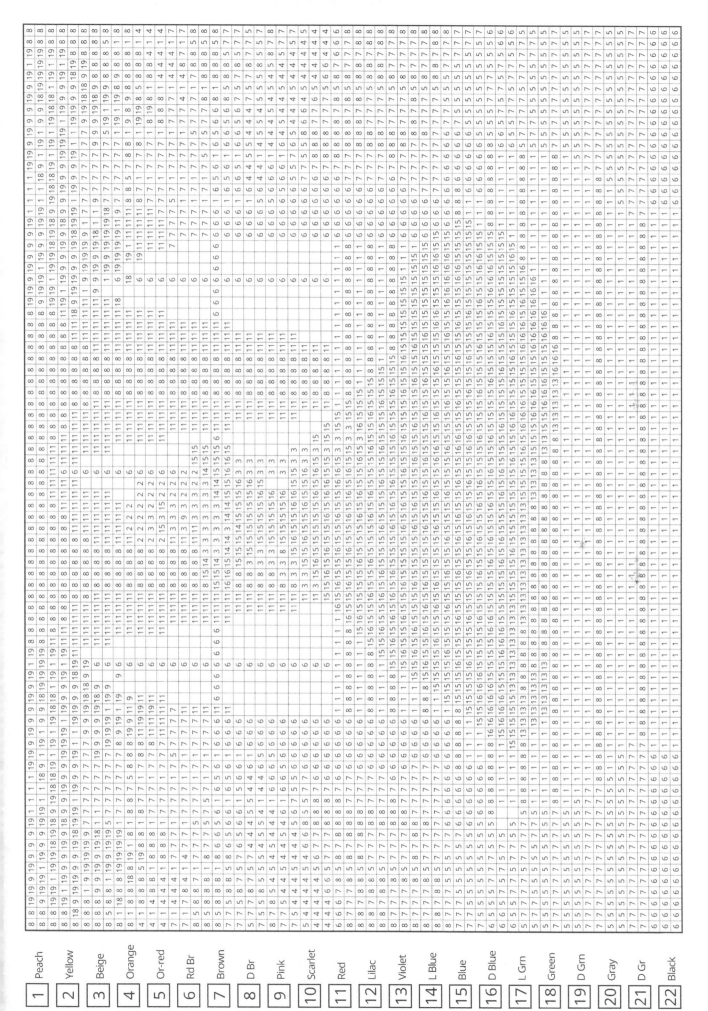

1	Peach
2	Yellow
3	Beige
4	Orange
5	Or-red
6	Rd Br
7	Brown
8	D Br
9	Pink
10	Scarlet
11	Red
12	Lilac
13	Violet
14	L Blue
15	Blue
16	D Blue
17	L Grn
18	Green
19	D Grn
20	Gray
21	D Gr
22	Black

Women are naturally secretive, and they like to do their own secreting.

Arthur Conan Doyle

If I'd observed all the rules, I'd never have got anywhere.

Audrey Hepburn

1	Peach
2	Yellow
3	Beige
4	Orange
5	Or-red
6	Rd Br
7	Brown
8	D Br
9	Pink
10	Scarlet
11	Red
12	Lilac
13	Violet
14	L Blue
15	Blue
16	D Blue
17	L Grn
18	Green
19	D Grn
20	Gray
21	D Gr
22	Black

All you need in this
life is ignorance and
confidence, and then
success is sure.

Mark Twain

1	Peach
2	Yellow
3	Beige
4	Orange
5	Or-red
6	Rd Br
7	Brown
8	D Br
9	Pink
10	Scarlet
11	Red
12	Lilac
13	Violet
14	L Blue
15	Blue
16	D Blue
17	L Grn
18	Green
19	D Grn
20	Gray
21	D Gr
22	Black

Friendship isn't a big thing — it's a million little things.

Mark Twain

1	Peach
2	Yellow
3	Beige
4	Orange
5	Or-red
6	Rd Br
7	Brown
8	D Br
9	Pink
10	Scarlet
11	Red
12	Lilac
13	Violet
14	L Blue
15	Blue
16	D Blue
17	L Grn
18	Green
19	D Grn
20	Gray
21	D Gr
22	Black

Keep smiling, because life is a beautiful thing and there's so much to smile about.

Marilyn Monroe

1	Peach
2	Yellow
3	Beige
4	Orange
5	Or-red
6	Rd Br
7	Brown
8	D Br
9	Pink
10	Scarlet
11	Red
12	Lilac
13	Violet
14	L Blue
15	Blue
16	D Blue
17	L Grn
18	Green
19	D Grn
20	Gray
21	D Gr
22	Black

Dress shabbily and they remember the dress; dress impeccably and they remember the woman.

Coco Chanel

Woman — like wind,
lightning, electricity.

Torri Higginson

1	Peach
2	Yellow
3	Beige
4	Orange
5	Or-red
6	Rd Br
7	Brown
8	D Br
9	Pink
10	Scarlet
11	Red
12	Lilac
13	Violet
14	L Blue
15	Blue
16	D Blue
17	L Grn
18	Green
19	D Grn
20	Gray
21	D Gr
22	Black

The strength of women comes from the fact that psychology cannot explain us. Men can be analyzed, women ... merely adored.

Oscar Wilde

1 Peach 2 Yellow 3 Beige 4 Orange 5 Or-red 6 Rd Br 7 Brown 8 D Br 9 Pink 10 Scarlet 11 Red

12 Lilac 13 Violet 14 L Blue 15 Blue 16 D Blue 17 L Grn 18 Green 19 D Grn 20 Gray 21 D Gr 22 Black

35

A girl should be two things: classy and fabulous.

Coco Chanel

1	Peach
2	Yellow
3	Beige
4	Orange
5	Or-red
6	Rd Br
7	Brown
8	D Br
9	Pink
10	Scarlet
11	Red
12	Lilac
13	Violet
14	L Blue
15	Blue
16	D Blue
17	L Grn
18	Green
19	D Grn
20	Gray
21	D Gr
22	Black

You educate a man;
you educate a man.
You educate a woman;
you educate a generation.

Brigham Young

A woman is like a tea bag; you never know how strong she is until she gets into hot water.

Eleanor Roosevelt

1	Peach
2	Yellow
3	Beige
4	Orange
5	Or-red
6	Rd Br
7	Brown
8	D Br
9	Pink
10	Scarlet
11	Red
12	Lilac
13	Violet
14	L Blue
15	Blue
16	D Blue
17	L Grn
18	Green
19	D Grn
20	Gray
21	D Gr
22	Black

Happiness is not a destination. It is a method of life.

Anonymous

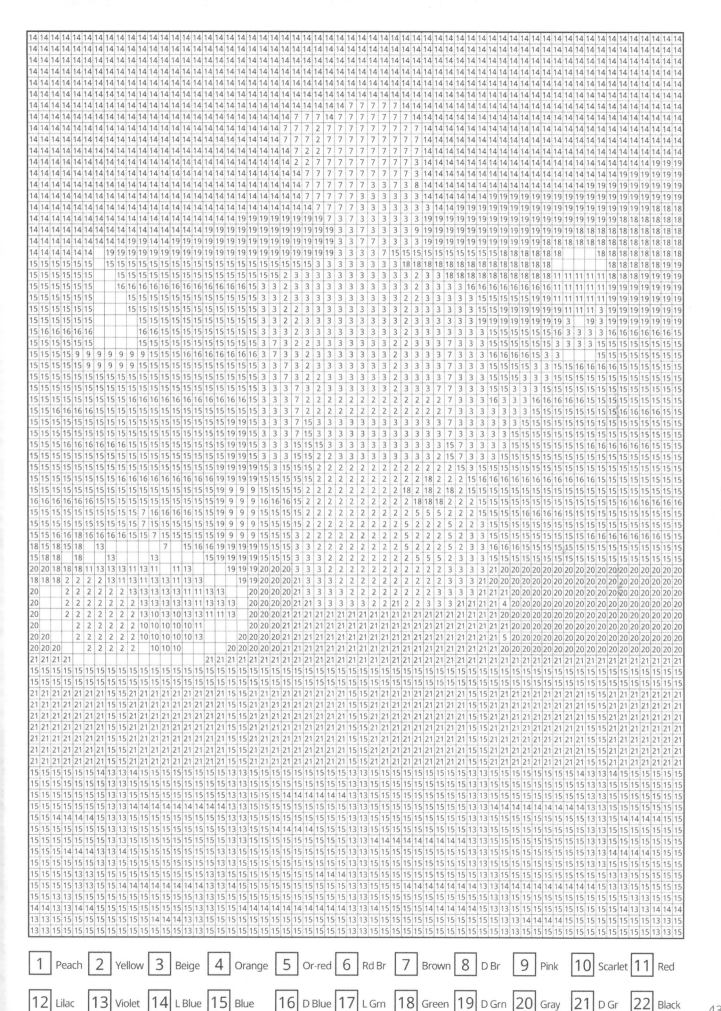

1	Peach	2	Yellow	3	Beige	4	Orange	5	Or-red	6	Rd Br	7	Brown	8	D Br	9	Pink	10	Scarlet	11	Red

12	Lilac	13	Violet	14	L Blue	15	Blue	16	D Blue	17	L Grn	18	Green	19	D Grn	20	Gray	21	D Gr	22	Black

*For some women it is
enough to walk down
the street once to remain
in the memory of a man
forever.*

Rudyard Kipling

1	Peach
2	Yellow
3	Beige
4	Orange
5	Or-red
6	Rd Br
7	Brown
8	D Br
9	Pink
10	Scarlet
11	Red
12	Lilac
13	Violet
14	L Blue
15	Blue
16	D Blue
17	L Grn
18	Green
19	D Grn
20	Gray
21	D Gr
22	Black

Modern paintings are like women, you'll never enjoy them if you try to understand them.

Freddie Mercury

1 Peach 2 Yellow 3 Beige 4 Orange 5 Or-red 6 Rd Br 7 Brown 8 D Br 9 Pink 10 Scarlet 11 Red

12 Lilac 13 Violet 14 L Blue 15 Blue 16 D Blue 17 L Grn 18 Green 19 D Grn 20 Gray 21 D Gr 22 Black

47

A hungry man is an angry man.

Proverb

1	Peach
2	Yellow
3	Beige
4	Orange
5	Or-red
6	Rd Br
7	Brown
8	D Br
9	Pink
10	Scarlet
11	Red
12	Lilac
13	Violet
14	L Blue
15	Blue
16	D Blue
17	L Grn
18	Green
19	D Grn
20	Gray
21	D Gr
22	Black

49

If women didn't exist,
all the money in the
world would have
no meaning.

Aristotle Onassis

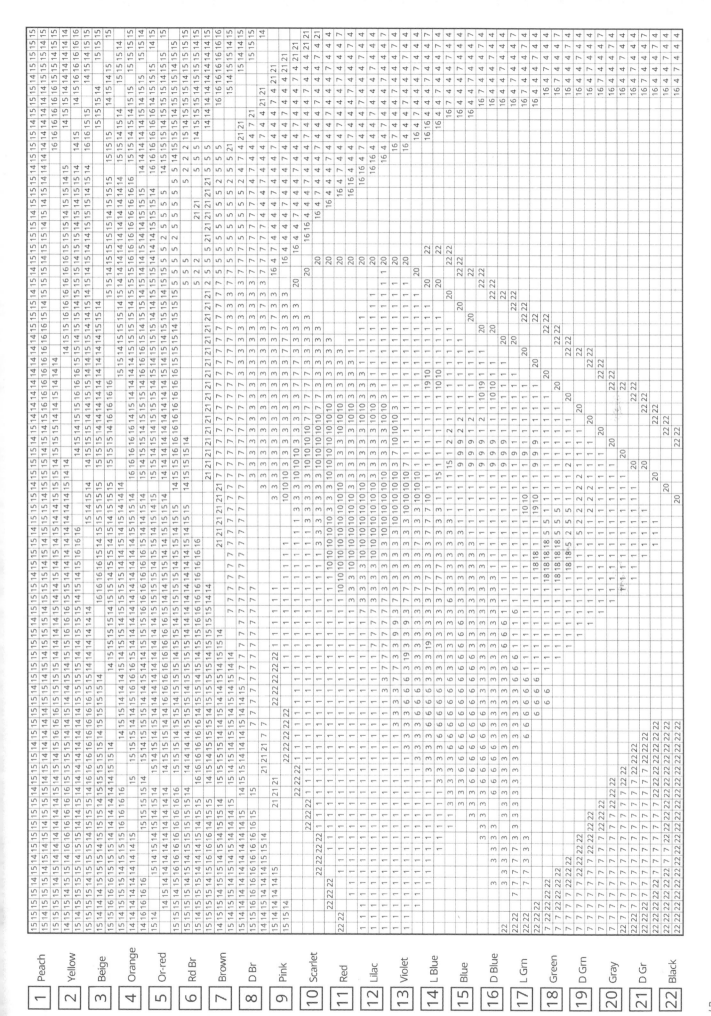

1	Peach
2	Yellow
3	Beige
4	Orange
5	Or-red
6	Rd Br
7	Brown
8	D Br
9	Pink
10	Scarlet
11	Red
12	Lilac
13	Violet
14	L Blue
15	Blue
16	D Blue
17	L Grn
18	Green
19	D Grn
20	Gray
21	D Gr
22	Black

All the world is made
of faith, and trust, and
pixie dust.

James Matthew Barrie

1	Peach
2	Yellow
3	Beige
4	Orange
5	Or-red
6	Rd Br
7	Brown
8	D Br
9	Pink
10	Scarlet
11	Red
12	Lilac
13	Violet
14	L Blue
15	Blue
16	D Blue
17	L Grn
18	Green
19	D Grn
20	Gray
21	D Gr
22	Black

WE ARE BELBA FAMILY.

All books are made with love for People and Nature.

We thank you for your choice.

And we will appreciate your feedback with a review of the book on Amazon, Facebook or Instagram.

Your opinion could help us to make our books better.

Follow us:

🅕 https://www.facebook.com/belbafamily/

🅞 Belba Family

Made in the USA
Columbia, SC
28 September 2022

68122274R00033